Drawing Is Fun!

DRAWING
SPEED MACHINES

011

D0503305

Gareth Stevens
Publishing

Please visit our website, www.garethstevens.com. For a free color catalog of all our high-quality books, call toll free 1-800-542-2595 or fax 1-877-542-2596.

Library of Congress Cataloging-in-Publication Data

Clunes, Rebecca.
Drawing speed machines / Rebecca Clunes.
    p. cm.— (Drawing Is fun)
ISBN 978-1-4339-5952-3 (pbk.)
ISBN 978-1-4339-5953-0 (6-pack)
ISBN 978-1-4339-5950-9 (library binding) --
1. Motor vehicles in art—Juvenile literature. 2. Speed in art—Juvenile literature. 3. Drawing—Technique—Juvenile literature. I. Title.
NC825.M64C58 2011
743'.89629—dc22

2010052703

First Edition

Published in 2012 by
Gareth Stevens Publishing
111 East 14th Street, Suite 349
New York, NY 10003

Cartoon illustrations: Dynamo Limited
Text: Rebecca Clunes and Dynamo Limited
Editors: Anna Brett, Kate Overy, and Joe Harris
Design: Tokiko Morishima
Cover design: Tokiko Morishima

Picture credits: All images supplied by Shutterstock.

Printed in China

CPSIA compliance information: Batch # AS11GS: For further information contact Gareth Stevens, New York, New York at 1-800-542-2595.

SL001844US

Contents

Bullet train

The front of this train is long and thin. This helps it to go faster.

The train is powered by electricity.

The train has a smooth shape. It can slip through the air easily.

The fastest bullet trains reach speeds of 200 miles (322 km) per hour.

FUN FACTS ● FUN FACTS ● FUN FACTS ● FUN FACTS ● FUN FACTS

It is possible to build faster bullet trains, but they are too noisy to use.

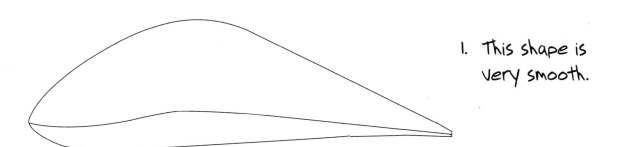

1. This shape is very smooth.

2. Draw the big windshield at the front. Show where the cars join.

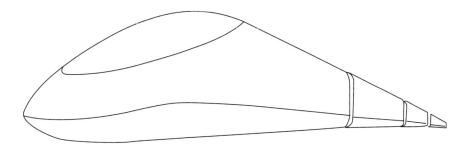

3. Now put in the rails.

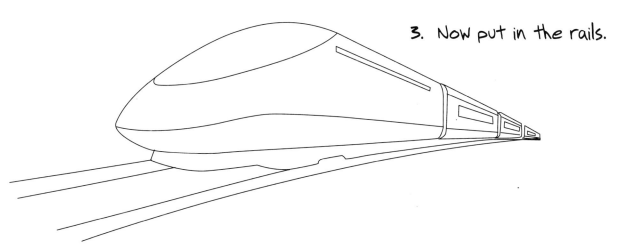

4. Now color in your train.

Race car

The back wing helps to keep the car on the road.

A race car has a powerful engine.

This car is very light but strong.

The tires are very wide. This stops the car from skidding.

FUN FACTS ● FUN FACTS ● FUN FACTS ● FUN FACTS ● FUN FACTS

The controls of the car are all on the steering wheel. The driver can find them quickly and easily.

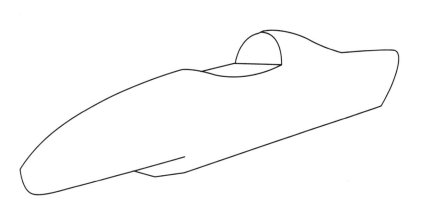

1. Here's another smooth, fast shape.

2. Add these shapes behind the driver's seat and at the front of the car.

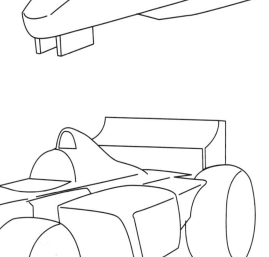

3. Now add some wheels and the wings at the front and back.

4. Red is a good color for a race car.

Speedboat

The windshield protects the pilot from the air rushing over the boat.

The powerful engine is at the back of the boat.

The front of the speedboat lifts up so it isn't touching the water.

FUN FACTS ● FUN FACTS ● FUN FACTS ● FUN FACTS ● FUN FACTS

The world record for the fastest speed on water is 317 miles (510 km) per hour. This record was set in 1978.

1. We can see the top and one side of this very pointy boat.

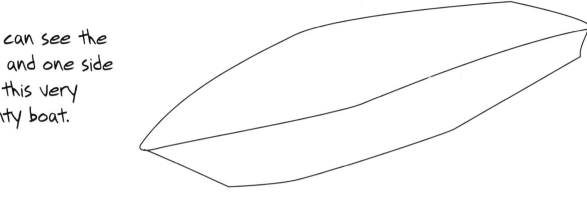

2. Add these shapes next.

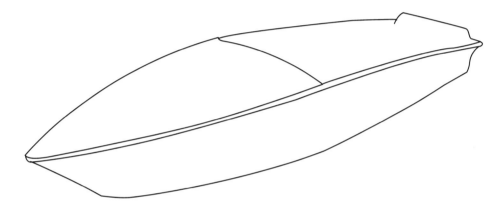

3. The windshield goes at the front.

4. Finish off the windshield and add an engine at the back.

Jet ski

Jet skis are small, fast, and easy to drive.

The driver sits here. A passenger can sit behind the driver.

The front of the jet ski pushes water away. The driver should not get too wet.

The engine pushes water out of the back.

FUN FACTS ● FUN FACTS ● FUN FACTS ● FUN FACTS ● FUN FACTS

The driver wears a cord attached to the boat. If he or she falls off, the cord is pulled out and the boat stops.

1. Draw this thin, flat shape for the bottom.

2. The soft seat goes in the middle.

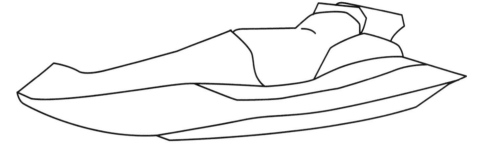

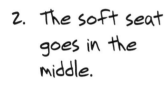
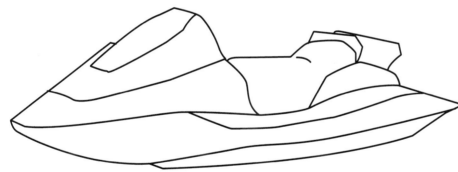

3. It's getting taller.

4. Give it handlebars like a motorcycle.

Stealth plane

The plane has four engines. They are inside the wings.

It has a pointed front. It can cut through the air easily.

There is only space for two people inside the plane.

The plane's shape makes it hard for enemies to tell where it is.

FUN FACTS ● FUN FACTS ● FUN FACTS ● FUN FACTS ● FUN FACTS

This plane can fly 7,000 miles (more than 11,000 km) before it needs more fuel.

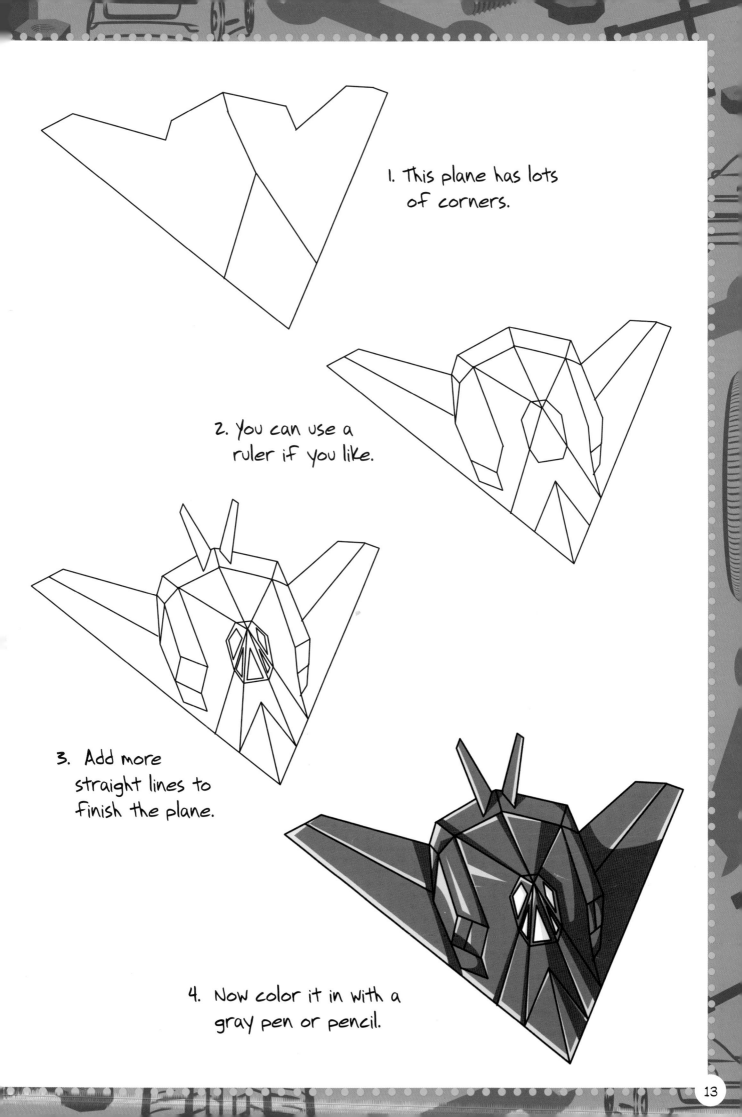

1. This plane has lots of corners.

2. You can use a ruler if you like.

3. Add more straight lines to finish the plane.

4. Now color it in with a gray pen or pencil.

ATV

The driver steers the ATV with handlebars, like a motorcycle.

ATVs can be driven over very bumpy ground.

They can move at 70 miles (112 km) per hour.

They have four wheels so they don't tip over.

FUN FACTS ● FUN FACTS ● FUN FACTS ● FUN FACTS ● FUN FACTS

ATV races can be on roads, over grass, on sand, and even on ice!

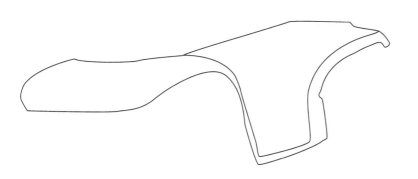

1. Draw the top of the ATV first.

2. Now put in the headlights and the seat.

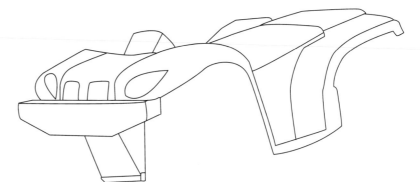

3. Put in the wheels next.

4. It has fat tires for driving over muddy fields.

Fighter plane

This plane can fly at 1,875 miles (3,017 km) per hour.

It can turn very quickly in the air.

The windshield is also a computer screen.

The pilot can see in all directions.

FUN FACTS ● FUN FACTS ● FUN FACTS ● FUN FACTS ● FUN FACTS

Fighter pilots must be hardworking, healthy, and strong.

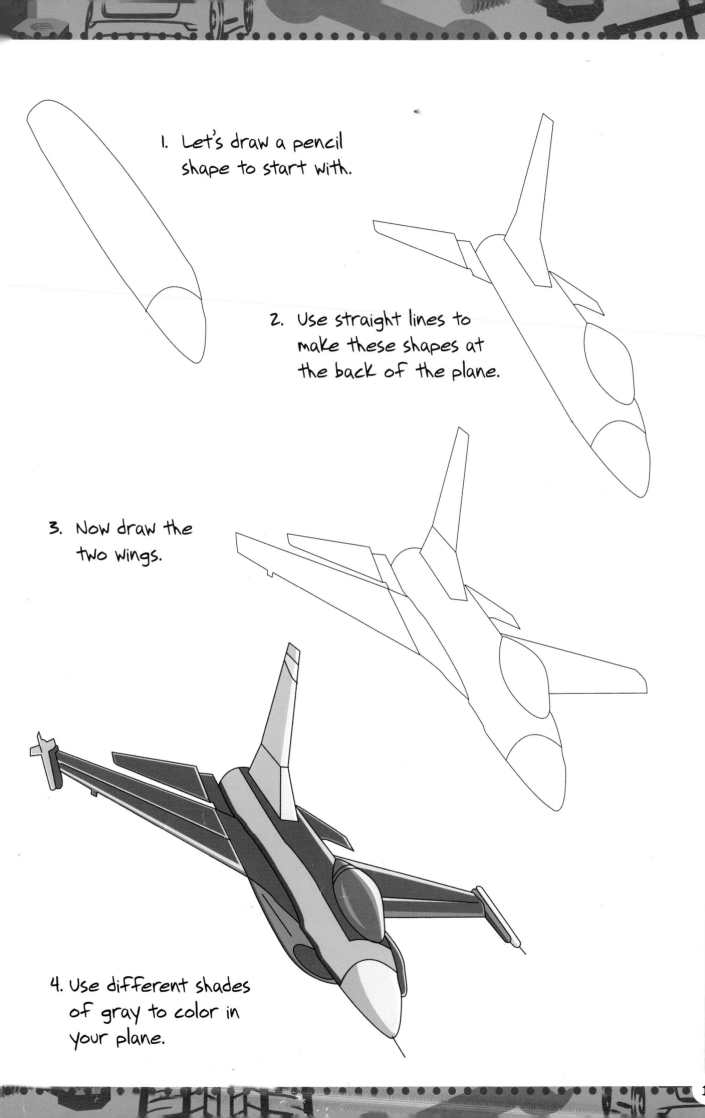

1. Let's draw a pencil shape to start with.

2. Use straight lines to make these shapes at the back of the plane.

3. Now draw the two wings.

4. Use different shades of gray to color in your plane.

Snowmobile

The snowmobile has headlights so that it can be used at night.

The engine turns a track at the back of the snowmobile.

This track can grip the slippery snow.

The skis at the front steer the snowmobile.

FUN FACTS ● FUN FACTS ● FUN FACTS ● FUN FACTS ● FUN FACTS

Some parts of the world are always covered in snow. Snowmobiles are the best way to get around.

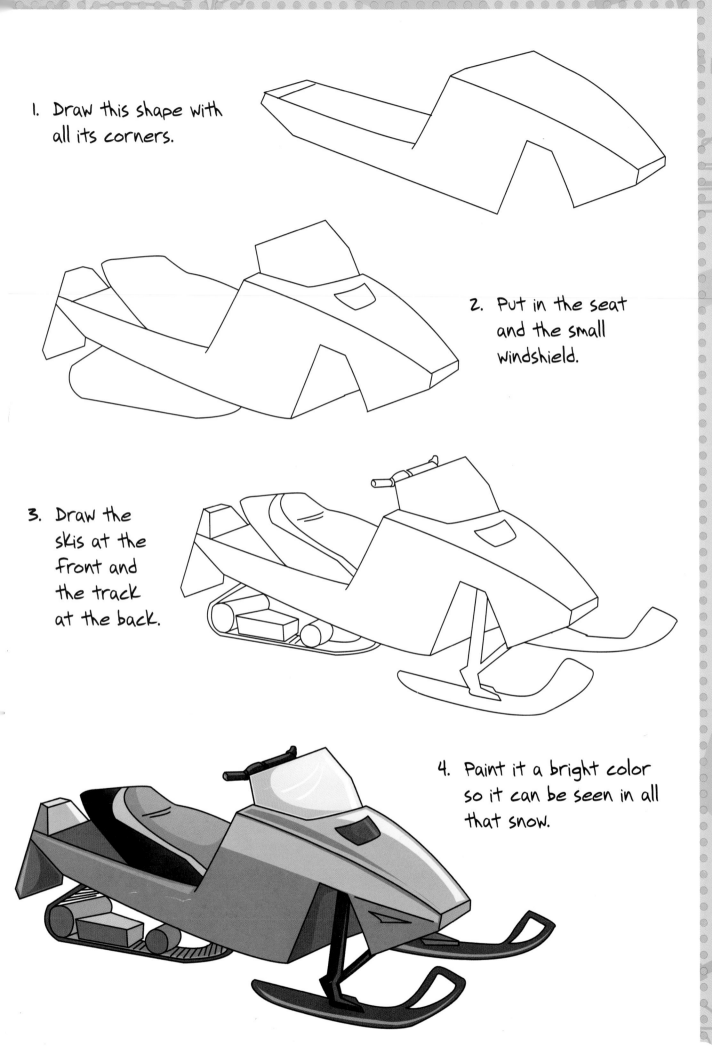

1. Draw this shape with all its corners.

2. Put in the seat and the small windshield.

3. Draw the skis at the front and the track at the back.

4. Paint it a bright color so it can be seen in all that snow.

Private jet

Flaps on the plane's wings control its speed and direction.

The engines are at the back of the plane.

This plane only carries about 10 passengers. It is very comfortable inside.

There are lots of windows so the passengers get a good view.

FUN FACTS ● FUN FACTS ● FUN FACTS ● FUN FACTS ● FUN FACTS

This plane can use short runways. This means it can land in places that bigger planes can't.

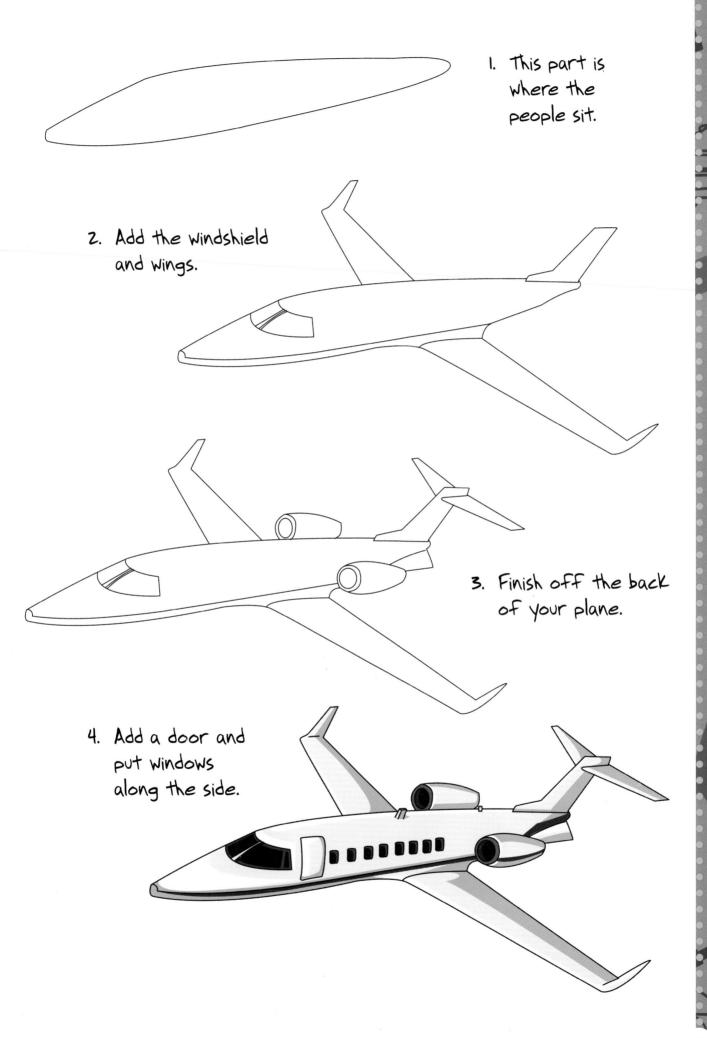

1. This part is where the people sit.

2. Add the windshield and wings.

3. Finish off the back of your plane.

4. Add a door and put windows along the side.

Kart

The engine is at the back of the Kart.

These pedals make the Kart go faster or stop.

Bumpers keep the driver from being hurt if a Kart crashes.

Karts have small, thick wheels.

FUN FACTS ● FUN FACTS ● FUN FACTS ● FUN FACTS ● FUN FACTS

Many top racing drivers began by racing Karts. There are races for Kart drivers as young as eight.

1. These shapes make up the front of the kart.

2. Draw in the wheels and add the steering wheel.

3. Next comes the seat and the back of the kart.

4. Color it in red and black.

Scooter

The front of the scooter protects the driver from dust and mud.

There is plenty of space to carry bags.

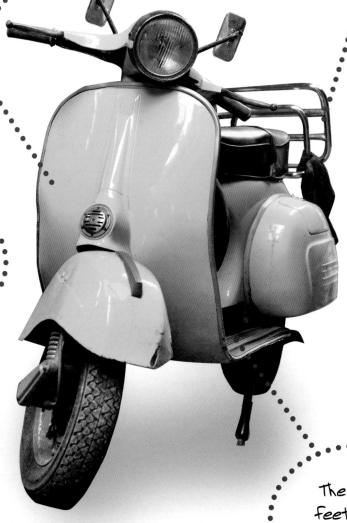

The small engine is at the back.

The driver's feet rest on this floor.

FUN FACTS ● FUN FACTS ● FUN FACTS ● FUN FACTS ● FUN FACTS

Scooters are great to drive in cities. They can keep moving while cars are stuck in traffic jams.

1. Start with this strange shape.

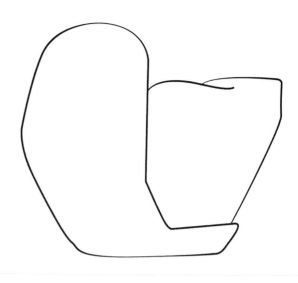

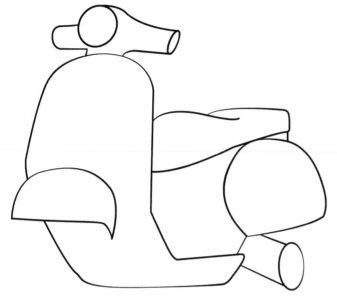

2. These lines make the seat and handlebars.

3. Now add the wheels.

4. Before scooting off, add lights and mirrors, and color it in.

Motorcycle and sidecar

A sidecar attaches to the side of a motorcycle. It means a passenger can come on the trip.

Some sidecars have a roof, but most do not.

A sidecar only has one wheel.

The passenger is very close to the road.

FUN FACTS ● FUN FACTS ● FUN FACTS ● FUN FACTS ● FUN FACTS

Sidecar races are very exciting. The passenger has to climb all over the sidecar and lean out around the bends.

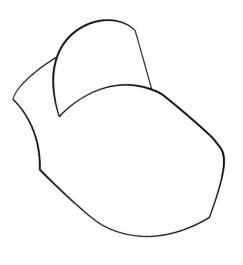

1. Use these shapes to start your motorcycle and sidecar.

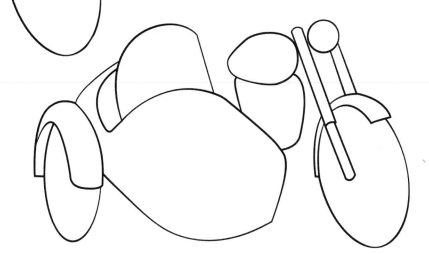

2. Begin to build up the motorcycle, and add a wheel to the sidecar.

3. Add the lights and handlebars, and draw more circles in the wheels.

4. Fill in the rest of the motorcycle and sidecar and color it in.

Stunt plane

A biplane has one wing on top and one wing below.

It has space for two people.

Biplanes have shorter wings than ordinary planes.

The propeller moves the plane forward through the air.

FUN FACTS ● FUN FACTS ● FUN FACTS ● FUN FACTS ● FUN FACTS

Planes with propellers are good at flying at slow speeds. People can easily see as the plane twists and turns in the air.

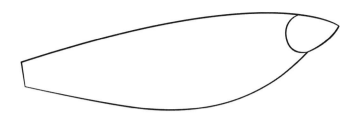

1. Start with a curved shape for the body.

2. Add in the two wings.

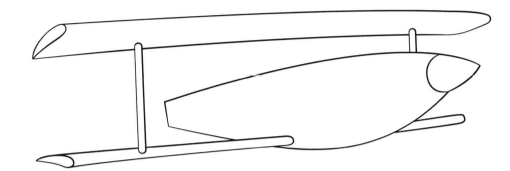

3. Now it's starting to look more like a plane.

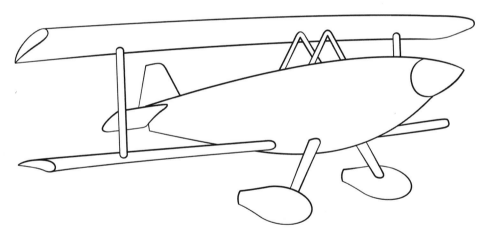

4. Add a propeller and choose bright colors to make the plane fly off the page.

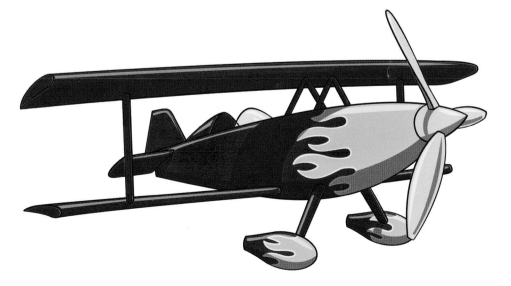

Sports car

The roof folds away with the press of a button.

This bar can carry the weight of the car if it rolls over in a crash.

There is only space for two people in this car.

These holes take air to the engine to help it work.

FUN FACTS ● FUN FACTS ● FUN FACTS ● FUN FACTS ● FUN FACTS

This car has a top speed of almost 200 miles (322 km) per hour.

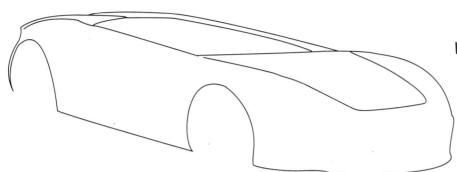

1. This car shape is very curved.

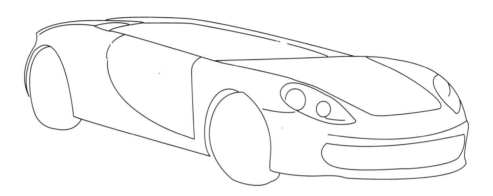

2. See how the wheels tuck into the body.

3. Add the windshield and the passenger seat.

4. Now your car is ready to color in.

Glossary

bumper something that protects a vehicle in a crash

cord a thick piece of string

engine a machine that makes a car, boat, or plane go

handlebars the part of a motorcycle that you hold to steer

headlights the bright lights at the front of a vehicle that are used to see at night

passenger a person who is in a vehicle, but who is not driving

pedal part of a machine that is controlled by pushing with your feet

pilot the driver of a plane or a boat

propeller a machine that has blades that turn around. It moves a plane or boat forward

runway a smooth level path where airplanes take off and land

skis long, narrow pieces of wood or plastic that move easily over snow

track a belt that moves a vehicle over the ground

vehicle a car, boat, plane, or other machine used to move people around

windshield the window in front of the driver

Index

Further Reading

Ragsdale, Linda. *Cars, Trucks, Trains & Planes You Can Draw*. Lark Books, 2008.

Rashidi, Waleed. *NASCAR Learn to Draw Race Cars*. Walter Foster, 2006.

Sexton, Brenda. *You Can Draw Planes, Trains, and Other Vehicles*. Picture Window Books, 2011.